LESSONS LEARNED ON THE SEAT OF MY BIKE

—Volume 2—

LESSONS LEARNED ON THE SEAT OF MY BIKE

- Volume 2 -

SECRETS
to successfully navigate your life's course!

PAUL WAGLER

© Copyright 2015 – Paul Wagler
All rights reserved.

This book may not be copied or reprinted for commercial gain or profit. Scripture quotations are from the New International Version of the Bible, unless otherwise indicated.

Cover Design by Angie Wagler
Thanks to Editing Team:
Angie Wagler, Don Boyd
and Jim Loepp Thiessen for your helpful suggestions.

ISBN-13: 978-1519744722
ISBN-10: 1519744722

ENDORSEMENTS

Paul Wagler has done it again! A dynamic follow-up to his first book, *Lessons Learned on the Seat of My Bus: Secrets to Enjoying Life No Matter What Happens!*, you'll enjoy how Paul delivers life-changing lessons for avid cyclists, non-riders, mountain bikers, fair-weather riders, and everyone else in between.

Ride along with Paul as he authentically shares the joys, the pains, the victories, and the mistakes he has experienced—on and off these non-motorized two wheels—so that you can gain gold nuggets about living a life that matters, pressing on, and finishing well. You'll even discover why you don't want a DNF or a DNS beside your name. Enlightening, practical and thought-provoking, well worth the read.

- *Jackie Morey, COO of Customer Strategy Academy*
 www.Your21stCenturyBusinessCard.com
 www.CustomerStrategyAcademy.com
 www.Your90DayLaunchpad.com

Paul's life can serve as an example for all of us. His use of stories from his biking experiences, to illustrate simple yet deep truths, is outstanding. He takes the complex and makes it simple. His book is a must read.

    - *David Powers, Author and Coach*
    www.fear-to-faith.com

I enjoyed reading Paul's book. He has biking illustrations that fit pretty much all of life! And they are great illustrations! I feel myself limping with him as he runs in his bike shoes to the finish line! It's amazing!!

    - *Jim Loepp Thiessen, Pastor*

THANKS TO:

—My lovely wife Angie

For your support and encouragement—it has been incredible! I am so appreciative of your hard work, time and talent that have helped Two Wheel Racing become what it is. You always make us look good! And for your dedication in making this book a reality.

—My children, Jamie, Melissa & Samantha

Many hours have been spent together riding, racing and travelling. I treasure those times. You all certainly make our family times together memorable. I have felt incredibly blessed to be able to spend the many hours I have with my family pursuing this passion of cycling.

—My brother, Duane

I'm so glad for our shared passion of riding our bikes. Thanks for your friendship, support and our brotherly rivalry in races to see who's faster on race day!

—All members of Two Wheel Racing —past and present

Your dedication, passion and ongoing friendships are inspiring to me. Thanks for sharing the journey and making so many special memories. As one former member use to say "Bom-Chicka-Wah-Wah!"

TABLE OF CONTENTS

Preface..11

Introduction..17

Chapter 1 - Enter...27

Chapter 2 - Equipment......................................41

Chapter 3 - Eyes...59

Chapter 4 - Encouragement..............................71

Chapter 5 - Eat..81

Chapter 6 - Endure to the End.........................101

Chapter 7 - Evaluate..123

Conclusion...129
More About Paul & Angie Wagler....................133
One Last Thing..135

PREFACE

As I go through life I am always thinking about what I can learn from the things that I experience every day. It seems this is just the way I am wired. What can I learn from what is happening in a way that will benefit me as a person? As I often speak in churches, I'm also wondering how I can use these life lessons as examples in my sermons.

In the Bible, Jesus regularly taught using examples of things from everyday life that people could relate to. He would say, "The Kingdom of God is like a man who went out to sow seed," or "the Kingdom of God is like a man who had two sons." We call these stories, "parables." A parable is an earthly story with a heavenly meaning.

This book about what I have learned on the seat of my bike is a modern-day parable. I like to think that, if there were mountain bikes 2,000 years ago, Jesus might have said, "The Kingdom of God is like the man who went out to race his mountain bike."

Several years ago, I was asked by a good friend to speak to a group of men. The topics I was to speak on were our bike team, my faith, and how they were connected. Within a short time, the framework of how to present this came to me. Since that first time I have had the privilege of sharing this talk several times. Now, this talk has become the book that you are about to read.

There is much that can be learned about life, from a race. Several times in the Bible being a follower of Jesus is compared to a race.

Preface

Hebrews 12:1-3

Therefore, since we are surrounded by such a great cloud of witnesses, let us throw off everything that hinders and the sin that so easily entangles. And let us run with perseverance the race marked out for us, [2] fixing our eyes on Jesus, the pioneer and perfecter of faith. For the joy set before him he endured the cross, scorning its shame, and sat down at the right hand of the throne of God. [3] Consider him who endured such opposition from sinners, so that you will not grow weary and lose heart.

1 Corinthians 9:24-27

[24] Do you not know that in a race all the runners run, but only one gets the prize? Run in such a way as to get the prize. [25] Everyone who competes in the games goes into strict training. They do it to get a crown that will not last, but we do it to get a crown that will last forever. [26] Therefore I do not run like someone running aimlessly; I do not fight like a boxer beating the air. [27] No, I strike a blow to my body and make it my slave so that after I have preached to others, I myself will not be disqualified for the prize.

Lessons Learned on the Seat of My Bike

2 Timothy 4:6-8

⁶ For I am already being poured out like a drink offering, and the time for my departure is near. ⁷ I have fought the good fight, I have finished the race, I have kept the faith. ⁸ Now there is in store for me the crown of righteousness, which the Lord, the righteous Judge, will award to me on that day—and not only to me, but also to all who have longed for his appearing.

These verses provide the foundation for this book that you are about to read. As I have lived my life, I have realized that, in many ways, I am in a race that sometimes feels like a battle or competition. I have found these verses to be quite encouraging in the midst of this race. It is my hope that, as you read this book, you will be encouraged in your life of faith—to continue running the race of trusting God, in the midst of whatever you are facing. If you are not a follower of Jesus, my hope is that you will consider the potential that faith has to offer in the race of life.

Preface

I will elaborate more on the thoughts expressed in these passages throughout this book.

INTRODUCTION

I love riding my bike! Actually, I love riding all my bikes; I own several of them! I'm not sure if I can pinpoint exactly why I love doing this so much. Is it the feel of the wind in my face? (I say "wind in my face" as opposed to "wind in my hair" as I'm wearing a helmet and I'm bald!) Is it the freedom I feel as I ride down the road or trail? Is it all the wonderful places my bike has taken me? Or is it the amazing destinations I have taken my bike? Maybe it is the mystery of how one can balance something with only two wheels without falling over? Is it all the health benefits that come from the regular exercise? Is it all the friends I have met riding my bike? Is it the energy and excitement that comes from racing? Maybe it's the thrill of riding a technical section of trail successfully on my mountain bike! Or could it be the sense of accomplishment from riding up a very long climb or doing a marathon ride or race?

Most likely, it is a combination of all these things that I have listed. Riding a bicycle, in some ways, is one of the simple things of life. As the expression states—"It's like riding a bike." This is usually said when referring to something you have learned how to do and will never forget. Even though riding a bike is simple or basic in a lot of ways, the effects of a bicycle on a person's life and the whole of society can be quite astonishing. I know my life has been dramatically changed as a result of pursuing this passion for riding. For this I am very thankful and will share stories of this change in my life throughout this book.

Introduction

There is something about pushing the pedals that brings a great level of enjoyment to me! I suppose that I have always loved doing this at some level. I remember as a little boy spending many hours on the farm where I grew up riding my bike— going off jumps, practicing wheelies and riding with no hands. For many years this passion was only a very casual part of my life.

In 2002, something changed. I had started a new job at Grand River Transit as a bus driver a year earlier. This job is very sedentary so the effect on me was some weight gain. I remember stepping on the scale after Easter dinner at my mother-in-law's house, (probably not the best time to weigh one's self) in the spring of 2002. I had hit an all-time high for me, in my weight; and it was then that I decided I needed to take some action. The following weeks I changed some of my eating habits and started riding my bike regularly. As the pounds started coming off, I felt very encouraged and started feeling much better physically as well. That summer my son, Jamie, and I signed up to participate in charity ride for Multiple Sclerosis. This was my first bike event, and I loved it. The ride was 75 km long; and, at that time, was a huge challenge. I remember how my legs hurt as we pedaled the last few kilometers, but we didn't quit. Finishing this first long ride at the MS Bike Tour got me hooked even more on riding my bike.

As I look back on the journey that I have been on since that first bike event in the summer of 2002, I am amazed at what has all happened in my life because of a bicycle. Thirteen years later, I have a garage that looks like a bike shop; I have competed in about 200 bike races; managed a mountain bike race team with my brother, Duane, and my wife Angie for the last 10 years. The team has several corporate sponsors. I've been all across Canada for rides and races, become a year round bike commuter, and have met many wonderful people who I am privileged

Introduction

to call friends and who share my passion.

How did all this happen? About the same time that Jamie and I were doing our first MS Bike Tour, Duane and his 3 boys were also getting interested in biking. They had all bought mountain bikes and had done a couple of mountain bikes races. At this time, the bike I owned was classified as a mountain bike but was actually more of hybrid. This Raleigh bike was also what we call rigid, in that it had no suspension. In the fall of 2002, I rode some mountain bike trails for the first time; and I didn't like it all. I wondered how anyone could like riding over all the roots and rocks! It was no fun at all for me!

I soon realized that having the right equipment for the type of riding you are doing makes all the difference. In 2003, after seeing the excitement grow for mountain biking within my extended family, I decided to buy a mountain bike with dual suspension. I bought a used Gary

Fisher Sugar 4 mountain bike from my local bike shop. I remember my first ride on the trails with this bike. Wow! What a difference the right bike for the job makes! On that bike, I now loved the mountain bike trails! Soon after this, I did my first mountain bike race; and I was hooked.

From 2003 to 2005, Duane and I, along with some of our children and a few of our nephews, did several mountain bike races each year. Our kids started to do very well in the races we entered. Many times, they would be finishing on the podium. With the success we were having and the growing interest in the sport, we decided to start a race team. "Two Wheel Express" was launched in 2006 with some limited sponsors. Two years later, in 2008, we were very fortunate to receive sponsorship from Recharge with Milk. This is a program with the Dairy Farmers of Canada to promote chocolate milk as a sports recovery drink. Duane and I made a pitch to them about how we could promote chocolate milk in the

Introduction

mountain bike race community. They decided to sponsor us, and we then helped to organize chocolate milk giveaways to racers at the finish line at several races each year. These became very popular races, and we became known to some as "the chocolate milk team". Eight years later, Recharge with Milk is still sponsoring our team; and we love promoting chocolate milk!

Also, in 2008, we started a sponsorship with Devinci Bicycles, which lasted for two years. In 2010, we switched to Scott Bikes for our teams' bikes and are still sponsored by Scott today. As well, our team, Two Wheel Racing, (the name changed in 2011) is privileged to be sponsored by Continental Tires and Fizik. We also have been supported for many years by several local businesses that have helped our team support our members to pursue their goal of being the best they can be. Over the years we have had several riders achieve great success on a Provincial and National level. Twice my nephew, Tyson Wagler, has represented Canada at the World Mountain Bike Championships. My daughter, Samantha, has raced in several World Cups races as well.

I love race day! It has become something that I look forward to and enjoy very much. There is a routine to it that I have developed over the years of racing. There are the foods that I like to eat and the times to eat them. There is the packing of the vehicle that I will be driving to the race with all the necessary gear for the day. I like to arrive at the race in plenty of time so that the time leading up to the race can be relaxed and not rushed. Our team has a trailer and several tents that we set up at races. This is the place where the team gathers before and after the race. In most races, I have already preregistered before race day; but I always have to sign in upon arrival at the race.

After a warm-up ride it is time to do the race. After the race, there is always a time of talking with other racers to compare our race stories.

Introduction

One of the best parts of the day is refueling with some chocolate milk and some good food. Then it is time to pack up the trailer and our vehicles and head for home. Finally, at home, I have to unload all the things I carefully packed earlier that day. I have done this routine many times over the last few years.

As I have ridden my various bikes thousands of kilometers training, commuting and racing. I have learned many things, not only about cycling, but also about life in general. In the pages that follow, I will share from these experiences with the hope that, as you read, you will be encouraged and challenged in your life's journey.

I also hope that many of you will be inspired to dust off that bike that has been sitting in your garage or basement. Or maybe you will need to go out and buy a bike. Either way I hope that you find the joy that comes from the simple act of riding a bicycle.

Chapter 1
ENTER

A mountain bike race is usually a family event! This is one of the things that I love about the sport! Often, people come as families with several family members all participating in the race. The atmosphere is friendly and welcoming to all. Many of the people that are there to watch or support others are mountain bike riders but, for one reason or another, have decided not to race. Some of these people talk about doing a race sometime but, for some reason, never seem to sign up for the race. Sometimes, these mountain bike riders will pre-ride the race course the day before the race with us but still will not be on the start line on race day.

Sign In

Now, mountain bike racing may not be for everyone; but if you want to be in the race, there is one thing that you must do. You can't just show up at the start line and say, "I want to do this race." No, you must officially ENTER the race. You need to sign up. This is called registering for the race, and, in most cases, is done online well before the race; although, sometimes, there is an option to sign up on race day.

Regardless of whether I have registered for the race before race day or not, when I get to the race I need to sign in. The race organizer wants to know, not only who has registered, but also who is actually going to show up for the race!

Chapter 1 — Enter

Many times, there are people who sign up for races; but they don't show up on the start line. I suppose this can be for a number of reasons, like injuries or family emergencies; but in our sport, many times, people decide not to race based on the weather. We like to call these people the "fair-weather riders." Mountain bike races go rain or shine. I much prefer the sunny, dry days, although we do have some great memories and stories from the rainy and muddy days.

Number Plate

When we sign in at a race, we are given a number plate to attach to our bike. Sometimes, in addition to the number plate on our bike, we are given numbers to attach to the back of our jerseys. This varies from race to race, but the main thing is for the race organizer to have a way to know who you are. Often, the racer is given some kind of timing chip as well to help keep track of results. This can be in the form of a something you strap around your ankle; or, lately, it has often been a strip on the back of the number plate we attach to the bike. If I show up at the start line without a number plate, I won't be participating in the race.

A friend of mine was doing his first triathlon a few years ago. He registered for the race and signed in on race day. Somehow, he had missed the instructions about the timing chip he was supposed to put on his ankle. He completed the race but there was no record of him even being in the race in the results! How disappointing to have competed in a race only to find out you actually weren't in the race according to the organizer!

I have another friend who was out for a ride on his road bike one day and ended up riding on a road that was part of a race that was in progress. He joined in with a large group of riders and enjoyed the benefits of riding in a group for several kilometers. My friend then left the group

Chapter 1 — Enter

and continued his ride on his own. If he had continued to the finish line he would not have been recognized as one who finished the race, as he hadn't registered for the race.

So what does all this information about entering mountain bike races have to do with the rest of life? What can we learn from this process that applies to how we live each day?

Changes

Many people who have signed up to do a race have found that just deciding to register for the event changes their life. There is something that motivates you to prepare for the event once you have committed to do it. This is why many people choose to race regularly or even just occasionally. Knowing that you have a race coming up motivates you to train, even when you don't feel like it. I will go for training rides when I would rather have a nap or when the weather is not very favorable at all because I have a race coming up.

I have also seen how this can cause someone to make drastic changes in their diet, as well; all to prepare for a race. A few years ago my daughter, Samantha, and I signed up to do a 3-day Stage Race called "Crank the Shield." We had registered to race as a two-person team. That means we would ride the whole race together over the course of 3 days. A few weeks before the race, Samantha was concerned about how prepared, or, shall I say, unprepared, I was for this race. She suggested (or perhaps demanded) that I make some adjustments to my diet in the weeks leading up to the race. The request was for me to have no ice cream for several weeks leading up to the race. Wow! I love ice cream and like to have some regularly; but because I was committed to doing this race, I made the sacrifice. I was motivated, not just for myself, but because I had a race partner. My preparation, or lack thereof,

Chapter 1 — **Enter**

would not just affect me but also Samantha.

An interesting, little thing happened to me during this time of no ice cream. We were away as a family, taking in the World Mountain Bike Championships at Mont-Ste-Anne, Quebec. After a meal out, on the way back to the hotel, everyone in the car wanted a dessert treat to top off the meal. I stopped and bought a container of ice cream to take back to the hotel for my family to eat. Wasn't that nice of me to buy everyone some ice cream to eat when I couldn't have any? When we got to the hotel Angie and the three kids sat down to eat the ice cream; and I left, as I had to attend to some other business. When I came back, they said they had left me some ice cream; and Samantha was lifting her imposed ice cream ban. I thought this was great, as I would finally get to taste some ice cream after a VERY long time without any. I got a bowl out and got the ice cream out of the freezer. I thought by the weight of the container they had left quite a bit for me to eat. Well was I surprised when I opened the lid to see the only thing in the container was ice cream-coloured water. There was no ice cream left at all—just water! They all had a good laugh at the prank they pulled on me. I maybe even chuckled a bit—maybe! So my diet of no ice cream continued for a couple more weeks. When the 3-day race was over, the first stop on the way home was to have some ice cream!

As I look back over my life, I can see how my life has changed, just from the decision to enter a race! This decision gave me a goal to work toward. I think that, as much as I enjoy doing the actual race, it is the effect that preparing for the race has on my life, that keeps me coming back for more. It all starts with the decision to enter the race! For me, this has been a practical example of the value of having a goal or vision and then committing yourself to do the work to bring it to pass.

I also see things we can learn from the

Chapter 1 — Enter

entering of a mountain bike race as it relates to being a follower of Jesus. As mentioned in the Preface, there are several times in Scripture that our journey as a Christian is referred to as a race.

Decision

The first key in following Jesus is the same as the first key in a successful race – you have to make a decision to join or enter. Perhaps you have heard the saying, "Going to church doesn't make you a Christian any more than standing in a garage makes you a car!" We could change that a bit by saying, "going to church doesn't make you a Christian any more than going to a mountain bike race makes you a racer!" At some point, we need to make a decision to enter the race or, in this case, become a follower of Jesus. It isn't enough to just hang around with other Christians. You need to "sign up" for yourself.

How do we enter this race or sign up to be a

follower of Jesus?

In the Romans 10:9-10, 13, we find some answers to this question.

> ⁹ If you declare with your mouth, "Jesus is Lord," and believe in your heart that God raised him from the dead, you will be saved. ¹⁰ For it is with your heart that you believe and are justified, and it is with your mouth that you profess your faith and are saved.
>
> ¹³ for, "Everyone who calls on the name of the Lord will be saved."

It all starts with believing in Jesus with all your heart. This belief, then, is so strong in our hearts that we declare that Jesus is Lord! To declare that someone is our Lord means that we have given control of our lives to that person. According to this Scripture, if there is this belief in your heart and confession from your mouth; you are now saved. You are now a follower of Jesus. It is that simple. It isn't complicated to sign up. Jesus has

Chapter 1 — Enter

done everything that needs to be done for you and me to become His followers. The gift of salvation is free for all who will receive it!

In all the bike races I do, I have to pay a registration fee to enter the race. One time, I had the privilege of doing a race where my registration fee was paid for me. It was awesome to go sign in on race day and know that someone else had paid my entry fee. This is what Jesus has done for you and me. He has paid the required registration fee, as it were, by his death on the cross so that we could be restored to relationship with God. He was the sacrifice for my sin and yours. In the words of the old song, "He paid a debt He did not owe. I owed a debt I could not pay. I needed someone to wash my sins away."

In a race, it is easy to identify who is in the race by the number plate on their bikes. When we decide to follow Jesus, the Bible tells us that we also are given a mark that identifies us.

Lessons Learned on the Seat of My Bike

Ephesians 1:13-14

¹³ And you also were included in Christ when you heard the message of truth, the gospel of your salvation. When you believed, you were marked in him with a seal, the promised Holy Spirit, ¹⁴ who is a deposit guaranteeing our inheritance until the redemption of those who are God's possession—to the praise of his glory.

When we believe, we are given the Holy Spirit, which marks us that we are now a follower of Jesus! We have entered the race! If you are wondering who is a follower of Jesus, the answer is simple: Anyone that has the Spirit of God is a child of God.

I John 4:13 confirms this

¹³ This is how we know that we live in him and he in us: He has given us of his Spirit.

I love these verses that tell us how we are

Chapter 1 — Enter

given the Holy Spirit when we believe in Jesus.

There are two things I want to note here about mountain bike race results. Some racers have the letters DNF (did not finish) beside their name. We will deal with this later in the book. Some other racers may have the letters DNS (did not start) beside their name. This means they registered for the race by paying the registration fee but didn't show up for the race.

So, even if we decide to sign up to follow Jesus, we still need to "show up" for the race. This happens each day when we decide to actively live our lives as followers of Jesus. There have been many who have decided to become a Christian but, for one reason or another, have never moved past that decision. They have continued living their life the same way they did before they made that decision. If we are truly followers of Jesus, then our lives will change from what they used to be. We cannot stay the same with the Spirit of

God now dwelling in us.

Just as doing a mountain bike race all starts with the decision to register for the race, so to being a follower of Jesus begins with a decision. Movement in our life begins with a decision. Choose well!

> *Reflection:*
>
> - What decisions have you made that have changed your life?
>
> - Is there an area where you are struggling to make a decision to move ahead?
>
> - What is one step you can take to start the process?

Chapter 2
EQUIPMENT

The success of every mountain bike race is determined by several factors. In my mind, the two most important, of all the variables that can influence your race, are the condition of your bike and the condition of your body. In this chapter we will focus on the bike.

Taking care of your equipment is one of the most important things you can learn as a mountain bike racer. Over my years as a racer, I have seen the outcome of a race be determined many times because of a "mechanical." That is the bike, for one reason or another, has stopped working in the way it was designed to; and the race for that rider is now over or severely hampered. This could be anything from a flat tire, a broken chain, chain suck, a broken frame, a chain coming off, the rear derailleur ripped off, a pedal falling off, the seat breaking off, the shifter not working, the handlebars breaking or wheels that can no longer spin because they got "tacoed" in a crash. I have literally experienced each one of these things or seen someone who has. I remember one time seeing a guy, whose race had ended early, carrying his bike with the frame snapped in two pieces. There are even more possibilities for problems than what I have mentioned, but this list gives you a good idea of what can go wrong.

Some of the problems you have with your mountain bike during a race cannot be avoided. For example you may end up in a crash that

Chapter 2 — Equipment

breaks something on your bike because someone trying to pass you clips your handlebar; or they may crash right in front of you, causing you to fall. These kinds of crashes can damage the bike, making it un-rideable or cause injury to the rider as well. This kind of situation is very disappointing as your race could possibly be over, through no fault of own!

Maintenance

The kind of bike failure in a race that I find even more disappointing is when the problem could have been avoided by doing some simple bike maintenance. When I started mountain bike racing I didn't know very much about maintaining my bike. My idea of maintenance was to occasionally check my tire pressure and lube my chain.

In the first race I entered after Two Wheel Express had become a team, I had a major mechanical in the first kilometer of the race. I was riding along and I thought something didn't feel right with my left pedal. Now, since I ride with bike shoes that clip into the pedal, my foot is attached to my pedal. Something felt loose, like I wasn't clipped into the pedal properly. While riding along, I was moving my foot around in order to get clipped in properly. All of the sudden, I looked down and the whole left crank-arm and pedal were not attached to my bike anymore; but my shoe was still attached to the pedal. I stopped the bike and then realized that I had lost the crank bolt that held the left crank-arm in place. I looked in vain on the ground to find the missing bolt. No one wants their race to end that way.

If I had known that it is a good idea to regularly check all the bolts on my bike, to make sure they aren't loose, this whole situation with my crank-arm falling off would have been avoided. I have seen many times, other racers have issues simply because a bolt came loose or fell out. This could

Chapter 2 – **Equipment**

mean a seat post that slides down, a handlebar that is loose, a shock that falls out, or a frame that comes apart because a suspension linkage bolt has come loose. Most of the time, these issues could all have been avoided by doing some regular bike maintenance.

Doing regular bike maintenance may not seem very appealing, but I have learned to enjoy taking care of my bikes. With regular use, the parts on a bike wear out and need replacing.

I remember the first time I changed the chain on my mountain bike. I went for a ride, and it was horrible. Every time I pushed hard on the pedals, the chain would skip, making riding very difficult. I wondered what is wrong. I thought changing the chain was going to make things better, not worse. I was learning a valuable lesson—if you leave a worn out chain on a bike too long, when you replace it, you will likely need to replace the chain rings (gears on the front) and/or the cassette (gears on the rear). So I ended up having to replace the chain rings and the cassette as well, after putting on my new chain. Now, I change my chain regularly and only occasionally have to change the cassette and chain rings.

Excess Weight

In the cycling world, the weight of your bike is also a big deal. When advertising a new bike, the bike company will usually list the weight of the bike with all the details of the components that are on the bike. There are riders I know that will try to make their bike as light as possible. This can be done by upgrading various components on your bike in order to save weight and hopefully enhance performance. When looking at new components for a bike, the weight of that part is listed in grams, so the buyer can see exactly how much weight they will be saving by buying this item. Some will have spent many hundreds, and even thousands of dollars on upgrades to their

Chapter 2 – Equipment

bike, just to save weight. We like to call these riders the "weight weenies".

As we talk of saving weight on a bike, the verse from Hebrews 12:1 comes to mind.

> Therefore, since we are surrounded by such a great cloud of witnesses, let us throw off everything that hinders and the sin that so easily entangles. And let us run with perseverance the race marked out for us.

The author of Hebrews encourages us to "throw off everything that hinders". In a bike race you want to have the lightest bike possible so you don't have to carry around the extra weight that hinders your performance in the race. Not only do you want to have a light bike, but you want your body to not carry around extra weight as well.

My approach has usually been rather than spending thousands of extra dollars on the lightest bike I will save money by eating less and getting rid of extra weight on my body. Either way, I am seeking to "throw off everything that hinders".

The image of strapping weights to your bike or body before is a race is rather ludicrous! No, we want to have nothing hindering us from doing our best in the race in which we are competing. The lighter we are and the lighter the bike is, the faster we will be able to ride. As we go through life, many times, we need to get rid of things that are hindering us in our journey.

What sort of things could be hindering us in our lives that we may need to throw off? It could be that your schedule is so full that you have no rest time, are lacking sleep, and never seem to get to do the things you really enjoy doing. Or maybe your time management is not very good and you are behind on "everything," which feels like a huge burden to carry. It could also be some habits that you have, or certain lifestyle choices

Chapter 2 — Equipment

you have made that may be hindering you.

As a follower of Jesus, there are many things that we can be involved in that are good. Many good things can fill up our time so much that we begin to feel distant from Jesus who wants to be our best friend. As in any relationship, if you don't spend time together, you grow apart.

I have heard it said that good is the enemy of the best. If we want to be faithful as followers of Jesus, we need to know what we are called to do and what we are not called to do. I have had to learn to say, "No," to some things that are good because my life was getting weighed down with too many things. The effect of too many things in my life was that important relationships were being impacted negatively. By putting into practice the words of this verse to "throw off everything that hinders," we can lighten our daily load and function better.

Entanglements

Another phrase in this verse that stands out to me is "the sin that so easily entangles". When I read this I am reminded of a mountain bike race I was in a few years ago. This race was called, "The Squeezer". Our team did this race every year for several years. I had gotten reasonably familiar with the racecourse after being a part of this event several times.

This one particular year, I remember that I had come up with a race plan that I thought would work really well for me. The first 4 km of this race was on pavement and gravel trails followed by single track sections. My goal was to be close to the front of the lead group by the time we reached the single track. Everything was going according to plan as we were riding along a gravel trail. I was close to the front, and we were almost at the single track. All of the sudden, my

Chapter 2 – Equipment

gears started to skip all over the place. Initially, I had no idea what was happening! I had never experienced anything like it before. I looked down at my gears, and I saw a long stalk of grass that, somehow, had got tangled up in my gears. I stopped my bike; and, thankfully I was able to pull this long grass out of my gears rather quickly.

In this case, my race wasn't over, but just delayed a bit. I lost quite a few places when I was pulled over pulling the grass out but was able to make up some of these places as the race went on. Needless to say, if I didn't stop and take the grass out of my gears, my race would have ended.

This is a good picture of what happens when sin comes into our lives. What is sin? I have heard various definitions, but there are two that I like the best. Sin is "simply missing the mark," or "the wanting and taking of your own way". When we sin, often we experience a "tangling" effect in our lives. Just like in the race when the grass in my gears prevented me from carrying on in the race, so sin has its effect on our lives. Maybe you have heard the old saying, "What a tangled web we weave when at first we do deceive". I think that sums it up well. Sin can slow us down in our race or even take us right out of the race. When we realize this, we need to stop and confess our sin.

The Bible tells us, in 1 John 1:9, that if we confess our sin, we will be forgiven. This is like when I stopped and removed the grass from my gears. After confessing our sin, we then need to make decisions that keep us from repeating this sin again in our lives. By continuing to make right choices in our lives we stay free from the entangling effect of sin.

Limit Screws

Another thing we can learn from the equipment on a bike comes from the derailleur—

Chapter 2 — Equipment

the part on a bicycle that is used to change gears by moving the chain from one gear to another one. Both the front and rear derailleur have two limit screws. They control the high and low range movements of the derailleur. When these limit screws are set properly the chain will not fall off when shifting gears. If the limits aren't set properly there is a very good chance the chain will come off at some point while riding. I have had this happen to me several times, and have learned, firsthand, the value of having limit screws properly set.

Sometimes, when the chain comes off, it can be a major problem. For example, if the chain comes off the top on the rear, it can become jammed between the cassette and the spokes. I have seen the chain be jammed so badly that it requires great effort to pull it out. If this happens in a race, it may not take you out of the race, but can greatly affect the end results.

In our lives, we also need to have our "limit screws" adjusted properly. A life that is lived without limits, may sound very appealing. It may even be seen as the ultimate goal; but, in reality, a life lived without limits is headed for some very tough times.

What are some limits that are important for us to have? We need to limit the food we eat, the money we spend, the numbers of hours we work and how busy our schedule is, just to name a few. Even as an avid cyclist, I need to limit the amount I train. There also needs to be limits properly set in our life as it relates to the words we speak. Choosing to speak kind and encouraging words, while making gossip and slander off limits, will save us from a lot of trouble. It will also enable us to be a consistent blessing to many people.

Ephesians 4:29 gives us some helpful advice about this.

Chapter 2 — Equipment

> Do not let any unwholesome talk come out of your mouths, but only what is helpful for building others up according to their needs, that it may benefit those who listen.

What a different world it would be if everyone limited the words they speak according to this verse. This one verse alone could change the world!

On a bicycle when the limit screws are properly adjusted, they are set given the current alignment of the derailleur. When you wipe out or crash while riding, sometimes the derailleur can be hit, causing it to go out of alignment. When this happens, often the chain will come off when shifting, as the current limit screw setting will no longer work. I have seen this happen to both front and rear derailleurs during a race. Often, it is when someone crashes and the bike lands on the right side. This can push the rear derailleur in a bit. You get up and start riding, but as soon as you get to a hill to climb, you go to shift to the easiest gear, and clunk! The chain comes off and is stuck between the cassette and the spokes.

How do you fix this problem you now have after a crash? The best thing to do is to realign the derailleur. Sometimes that can't be done right away, so a simple readjusting of the limit screws can be done to keep the gears working properly. There is also what we call a "farmer fix." This is simply giving the derailleur a good pull, with your bare hands. I have done this on a number of occasions as well.

Why am I explaining all this? I think this is a picture of what can happen very easily in our lives, if we aren't paying close attention. Sometimes, we may go through a rough time or a "crash" of sorts. This could be a major illness that we or someone close to us experiences. Or maybe it could be the death of a loved one. Perhaps it is a job loss or various kinds of relational problems, such as a marriage break up. These possible situations can

Chapter 2 — Equipment

all be summed up in this way.

> **Sometimes life doesn't turn out the way that we had hoped it would.**

When these things happen to us, the limits we used to function with might not work anymore. We may need to make changes to the previous limits that we had before the "crash".

Reflection:

I encourage you to think about your life right now.

- Are there areas of your life where you haven't had the limits set appropriately?

- Take the time you need to identify these and then make the necessary adjustments to set manageable limits.

I would also encourage you to think about your life from a maintenance point of view.

- How are you doing with your life's "equipment"?

- Are you going along just hoping everything will stay together and that nothing will break?

- Are you doing regular maintenance with your relationships and with your schedule?

- Are you paying attention to yourself and taking care of your physical body (We will talk more about this in a later chapter.), your emotional well-being, and your spiritual condition?

When I'm riding my bike I hate it when my bike makes noises it isn't supposed to make. Often, these noises are indicators that something is wrong and needs attention. Hopefully, in our lives, we can recognize these indicators as well and make the appropriate adjustments to avoid potential problems.

Chapter 3
EYES

I have received many tips over the years as a mountain biker from others who have more experience than me. I'm always grateful for this advice, as I know I have lots to learn. The top two tips I have received are how to avoid saddle sores on long rides (This one saves a lot of pain and discomfort!) and training my eyes where to look when I'm riding a trail.

In this chapter we will look at the tip about our eyes. As for the saddle sore tip it is simple—

on long rides always use some kind of chamois cream or lubrication on the part of your body that comes in contact with the seat of your bike. Your bottom side will thank you!

The Focus Rule

Look where you want to go!

"Your wheels will follow your eyes, so don't focus on what you want to miss"—easier said than done—especially if you are new to mountain biking. Your hands may be holding the handlebar; but, ultimately, it's your eyes that steer the bike!

If you have never been on a mountain bike trail, let me tell you about some of the possible obstacles there can be. There can be rocks of all sizes to avoid or ride over, trees, logs, roots, creeks, mud holes, bridges, ruts, steep ascents or descents, jumps, drops, and sharp corners on an uphill or downhill. The challenge is to navigate

Chapter 3 — **Eyes**

these technical sections of the trail successfully. Sometimes, this can take many attempts at a particular section until you conquer it.

This is one of the great appeals of mountain biking. The sense of accomplishment you get from being able to ride a section of trail or ride over an obstacle that previously you weren't able to is a great feeling. The first time I rode our local trails, many years ago, I was scared to ride some sections of trail that now seem easy. Every mountain biker can probably tell you a similar story of how they have improved with practice and helpful advice from others.

Over the years, I have crashed or seen others crash in technical sections of trail. This is not always the result of not having your eyes focused properly; but, many times, that plays a huge part in the crash. When the obstacles distract us, it is usually because fear is dominating our mind. Now, there is a healthy level of fear in mountain biking that will keep you riding within your limits or your level of skill; but, sometimes, we need to challenge that fear and break through to new levels of challenge. This is done when we focus our eyes on where we want to ride and don't get distracted by all the danger around us.

I remember doing a race, several years ago, on some trails that I had never been on before. There was one sharp corner in the race that was on the edge of a hill. I wouldn't say it was a cliff; but there was a definite drop off, if you didn't navigate this corner well. I approached this corner with some hesitation; and my eyes were focused more on the steep drop off beside the corner, than on the trail that I was trying to ride. I think you can guess what happened. I didn't make it through the corner on the trail but went off the trail and crashed. Thankfully, I didn't go very far down the hill when I wiped out. In this case, I was able to get back up, dust myself off, and continue the race.

Chapter 3 — Eyes

On another occasion, during a pre-ride of a race course, I did some major damage to my front wheel. There was a large rock on the course for us to ride over. As you rolled down off the rock, you needed to keep right to avoid hitting a tree. I had done this successfully a few times; but, for some reason, this particular time, I was focused on the tree. As I came off the rock, my eyes were drawn to the tree. Unfortunately, I rode straight into the tree with my front wheel taking all the impact. The wheel was completely destroyed from the collision. This was an expensive way to learn this lesson about training my eyes to focus where I want to go.

This lesson was, again, reinforced another time on a bridge over a swampy area in our local trails. I did not have a lot of experience, at this point, riding over bridges. This particular time, as I rode the 30-foot long bridge, I was looking more at the ground beside the bridge, exactly what I was trying to avoid. My eyes were definitely not as focused on the bridge as they should have been. I went off the bridge and went over the handlebars for a good spill. Thankfully, it was the middle of summer so the swampy area where I landed was dry.

Many times, I have seen the benefit of focusing my eyes on where I want to go and not on the obstacles or potential dangers around. This has helped me to be able to ride some sections of the trail that I would have never tried before. Currently, I consider myself a decent technical rider, realizing that there are many who can ride these challenging sections much better than I; but I have come a long way in my own skill from when I started out.

Another thing that is helpful with your eyes in mountain biking, is not to just look at the trail right at your front wheel, but look further down the trail. This will help you to ride the trail faster, as you're able to better prepare for what is coming

Chapter 3 — Eyes

up on the trail. When riding trails, the natural tendency is to look just in front of the front wheel. If we can train our eyes to regularly scan the trail 20-30 feet ahead, there is a noticeable difference in the speed that we are able to ride, especially through corners and technical sections.

What can we learn from this that connects with the rest of our life? Here are a few thoughts.

I once heard someone say, "What gets your attention gets you". In other words, we become what we focus on, or we go in the direction of the things on which we focus. As we go through life, there are many potential obstacles that we encounter along the journey. This can be a variety of things like relational conflicts, sickness and disease, financial difficulties, and major disappointments, just to name a few. Pretending that these challenges don't exist is not the solution, but neither is focusing so much on them that we don't see anything else. Somehow, in the midst of these times, we need to learn to look ahead to where we want to go, instead of being completely distracted and consumed by the problems that are around us.

Course Designer

Let's look again at this passage from Hebrews 12: 1b-2

> And let us run with perseverance the race marked out for us, [2] fixing our eyes on Jesus, the pioneer and perfecter of faith. For the joy set before him he endured the cross, scorning its shame, and sat down at the right hand of the throne of God.

As followers of Jesus, we are invited to "fix our eyes on Him". This is the key to running our race with perseverance. Jesus is the pioneer or the author of our faith. He is also the perfecter of our faith. What does all this mean? Let me explain with an example from mountain biking.

Chapter 3 — Eyes

A few years ago, the Ontario Provincial Championship race was held at a venue that had just built all new trails to host this event. As racers, we were all eager to try out these new trails before the actual race day. On one of these pre-ride days, I had the privilege of riding a lap of the course with two guys who had designed and built the trails. This is a rare opportunity—to be able to ride the trail with the fellows who built it!

As we were riding, they would say things like, "Go to the right of this rock," or "Aim for the groove in the rock when riding over it, and you will roll easily over the top," or "Make sure you keep up your speed in this section," or "Steep climb ahead," or "Don't go off this rock drop—take the chicken line". As I followed the advice of these trail builders, I found that difficult sections were made much easier. I was following these two guys on the trail so I could take the same lines they would take. I also had the helpful commentary from them as we rode. This made me think I wish I could do this on every trail I ride!

Jesus came to this Earth as a man. He was fully human, just like you and me. He went through the same things that we go through. Hebrews 4:14-15 says this:

> [14] Therefore, since we have a great high priest who has ascended into heaven, Jesus the Son of God, let us hold firmly to the faith we profess. [15] For we do not have a high priest who is unable to empathize with our weaknesses, but we have one who has been tempted in every way, just as we are—yet he did not sin.

The Scripture also tells us, in John 1:3, that, through Jesus, all things were made. So Jesus created this faith that we have. It was His idea. It is like He designed and built the trail. He then came and rode the trail and did it perfectly. Now, when we fix our eyes on Jesus, we get to follow the course designer, the course builder, and the best rider to ever ride this trail! How awesome is that!?!

Chapter 3 — **Eyes**

Fixing our eyes on Jesus as we go through life is the key to successfully navigating all the obstacles that come our way. Jesus is our best friend, and he has marked out the race for us. He gave us the example of how to live; and we have the Bible, God's Word to us, to guide us through life. Also, when Jesus returned to Heaven he sent the promised Holy Spirit to dwell in us to guide us every step of the way. We are not left alone but are well supported all along the journey.

I like how the verse in Hebrews says Jesus marked out the course for us. Some of the mountain bike racecourses I have been on are not marked very clearly. I have taken wrong turns at times and have seen others do the same. Sometimes, this has dramatically affected the outcome of a race. Sometimes, a wrong turn is made, simply because you were following the guy in front of you and he took a wrong turn. Taking a wrong turn in a mountain bike race can cause a lot of grief.

If we fix our eyes on Jesus, we will not go off the course. He will never lead us astray! If we take our eyes off of Him and end up off course, He is there, ready and willing to help us get back on track so we can carry on in the race.

Remind yourself of all these things daily with this simple phrase: "I choose to fix my eyes on You, Jesus!"

Reflection:

- Are you currently focused on problems that need solutions in your life?

- Are there fears that need to be managed?

- What steps can you take that will help to navigate your course without having these obstacles take you out?

Chapter 4
ENCOURAGEMENT

Go! Go! Go!

Up! Up! Up!

Push! Push! Push!

Or, as my friends from Quebec say, "Pousse! Pousse! Pousse!"

Keep going! You're doing great! Looking good!

Lessons Learned on the Seat of My Bike

These are all things you will hear at a mountain bike race, being shouted out to racers by fans that are there to cheer the riders on. Many times, these simple words that you hear as a racer give you an energy boost to go harder; or, sometimes, it's just that little something extra to just keep going.

I can recall times when I have been having a tough time during a race and someone along the racecourse cheers me on. I may not be having a good race and be very far back from the leader. I may even look as bad as I'm feeling. However, when someone says, "You're doing great," or "You're looking good," something positive happens to me. I feel a bit better and push the pedals harder. I even know that, sometimes, when I hear someone say, "You're looking good; keep going," what they are saying isn't true. I know I am really am not looking good, yet it still makes a positive difference in me. The effect of encouragement is incredible!

Chapter 4 — Encouragement

You may have seen on TV, at races like the Tour de France, where the fans are lining the course by the thousands. On the mountain stages, sometimes it is hard to see the road because there are so many fans cheering. I have experienced a small taste of this. In The Squeezer, a race that we used to do every year, the finish stretch was an uphill in the city of St Catharines. This was always lined with many people who would cheer frantically for every rider that came up the hill to the finish. Some years, there was even a guy dressed up as the devil like you see in the Tour de France. To ride up a hill that is lined with people cheering you on is an incredible feeling.

One year, at The Squeezer, I got a flat tire close to the end of the race. I thought I was about 1 or 2 kilometers from the finish, so I decided to not fix the flat but just run with my bike the rest of the way. It turned out to be somewhat longer than I anticipated. Bike shoes are not meant for running, and I don't train as a runner at all. I ride my bike—I don't run! By the time I got to the uphill before the finish line I was toast. My feet hurt, my legs were cramping, and I just wanted to walk slowly to the finish line. I came around the corner to climb the hill, and the crowd was cheering loudly. It seemed that people would cheer the loudest for the racers that were facing the most adversity. With all that cheering, something happened to me so that I was able to run all the way to finish line. Without the encouragement of the people lining the street this would have never happened.

Encouragement not only makes a huge difference in a bike race but also in the rest of life. It is something that we all need regularly to keep on keeping on. Encouragement, many times, is the difference between success and failure.

Let's look at the word 'encourage' closely. The word, encourage, has its origins from French. 'En' means 'to make' or 'put in'. Courage is a

Chapter 4 — Encouragement

quality of spirit that enables you to face danger or pain without showing fear. If we write the word 'encourage' as "in-courage" it may help to better understand it. When we give someone encouragement, we are actually giving them courage to continue and make it through whatever they are facing by rising above fear.

The opposite of this is the word, 'discourage.' How many of us are tired of having someone dis our courage? To 'dis' something is to show disrespect to, often by insult or criticism. I'm sure we would all agree, it is much better to be encouraged than discouraged.

In Hebrews 12:1, which we looked at in an earlier chapter we have this phrase:

> Therefore, since we are surrounded by such a great cloud of witnesses…

I love the picture this creates in our minds! As we go through life as a follower of Jesus, running the race that has been marked out for us, there are many who have finished the race that are cheering us on. When we face difficulties in life, or we want to give up, we can get encouragement from those who have run the race before us. When we hear the stories of these people, we receive encouragement to continue when we feel like giving up. We see how God has been faithful to them, and we know that He will be faithful to us as well. What an incredible blessing to be surrounded by this great cloud of witnesses!

Being Intentional

Not only do we need to receive encouragement to make it through life, but we also get to give it to others. Hebrews 10:24 is one of my favourite verses.

> And let us consider how we may spur one another on toward love and good deeds,

What a great picture is created here:

Chapter 4 — Encouragement

someone being spurred on to love and good deeds by another. I grew up on a farm, and what comes to my mind when I hear the phrase "spur one another on," is how we would spur the cattle on to go where we wanted them to go. When we would be loading cattle into a truck or moving them to a different pen, we would have a dog barking or nipping at their heels. Also, we would use our hands or a stick to tap them so they would be encouraged to move along. If the animals were left to just go wherever they wanted to, they would rarely if ever end up in the place we wanted them to go.

In the same way, you and I need those in our lives who will spur us on toward love and good deeds. We also get to give this encouragement to others. I love how this verse tells us to "consider how we may spur one another on"! This indicates to me that it isn't something that we are just to hope happens as we go through life. No, we are actually to think about ways to make it happen.

We are to make plans as to how we can encourage each other. What a different world we would live in if everyone gave thought, everyday, how they could encourage others and then followed through on these plans.

For some people being an encouragement to others seems to come naturally. It just seems to flow out of them to everyone they meet. These people tend to have a lot of friends, as everyone likes being around someone who is an encourager. I have also heard some people say, "Well, that's not my gift". I would suggest to you that, whether being an encourager comes naturally or not, it is something that we are all called to do. It is a gift that we all can cultivate and see grow in our lives.

How do we do this? It starts by simply considering, or giving thought to, or making plans to encourage one another. When we begin this journey, we will see the fruit of this in others;

Chapter 4 — Encouragement

and we are then encouraged to do it more. Encouragement becomes contagious. When you sow it into other people's lives, you will reap in your life as well.

I have come to love giving and receiving encouragement! I wouldn't be writing this book without the encouragement that others have given me that I have been given a message to share with others. I have seen the encouragement that I have given others enable them to soar to greater heights than they could have imagined. Encouragement is like fuel in a car. Without it, you won't go very far at all.

I have had people tell me that something I did or said was a great encouragement to them. Often this has been told to me years later. Many times, I had no idea that what I was doing would have the effect that it did. I have told others the same thing regarding the affect they have had in my life. If we practise encouraging others, it will soon flow out of us without us even realizing it!

I encourage you to look every day for someone who needs encouragement and then find a way to give it to him or her. Also, be open to receiving encouragement that others want to give to you. Sometimes, we dismiss or downplay the words others speak to us, thinking we aren't worthy of them. Receive these words and the blessing and strength they will bring into your life.

Reflection:

- Have you ever been helped by someone who encouraged you along the way?
- What did they do to encourage you?
- Have you ever thanked them?
- Who can you encourage today?

Chapter 5
EAT

I love to eat food! In fact, it seems that much of my life is planned around food. As soon as I'm done eating one meal, I am already thinking about the next meal. Sometimes I make plans days ahead, related to food and what I am going to eat. It is this love of food that played a big part in me getting started in cycling.

As I shared earlier in the book I had one of those life-changing moments when I stepped on the scale in 2002 and realized I needed to make some changes. At that point in my life, I weighed the most I ever had, so I decided to adjust my eating habits and started riding my bike. What a wonderful and transforming journey this has been!

Since that time, I have learned much about the foods that I eat and how they either help or hinder my performance on my bike. This learning is continuing to this day as I figure out what types of food to eat and when to eat them, in a way that will work best for me before, during and after a race. I don't claim to be an expert in nutrition in any way but have gained a very basic understanding of some things in this area. There are many things, written in other places, that will give you more detailed nutritional information, if that's what you're looking for. Here, we will just look at a few basics to get you thinking about these things.

As mentioned in Chapter 2, the two biggest

Chapter 5 – Eat

factors that determine how a race will go are the condition of the bike and the condition of the body of the person riding the bike. In this chapter, we will look at the body and how to fuel it for a race.

Fuel

Just as a car needs fuel in the tank to drive down the road, so the rider of a bicycle needs to have fuel in their tank to push the pedals. If we try to ride a bike without sufficient fuel in our bodies, we will eventually experience what is referred to as 'bonking.' Bonking is a state of overwhelming fatigue that occurs when the body's glycogen stores become seriously depleted.

What is glycogen? According to the American Heritage Dictionary, glycogen is defined as the main form of carbohydrate storage and occurs primarily in the liver and muscle tissue. It is readily converted to glucose by the body when needed to satisfy its energy needs.

In some circles, carbohydrates get a bad rap at times. In fact, there are some diets out there that seek to eliminate carbs completely or severely restrict them. Too many carbs without the right amount of exercise will, in most cases, lead to weight gain. For the type of racing that I do, carbs are essential to completing a race successfully.

I also want to mention here that having the right amount of protein in your diet is also crucial. Protein helps to repair our muscles after a ride or race. However, we can't function on carbs or proteins alone. There needs to be a good mix of both so I can do my best on race day.

Leading up to race day, I need to make sure that I am eating a good amount of carbs to keep my glycogen level high. If my glycogen levels are low going into a race, it likely won't matter how well I fuel my body during the race. I will not be

Chapter 5 — Eat

able to race to the best of my abilities because I have not prepared effectively for this race. To get the best results possible in a race, proper fueling or eating well is a lifestyle that you develop and not just something you do the day before a race.

Bonking

Several times over my years of cycling, I have experienced this thing called bonking. These times are memorable and not in a good way. In every case, the bonking could have been avoided if I had fueled my body properly and sufficiently. Sometimes this has happened on long training rides where I ran out of food and/or drink and didn't have an option to get more.

Just this past summer, I was out on a training ride on my road bike; and the weather was great. I was feeling good, so I decided to go take a route I had not done before. The length of this ride ended up being around 90 km; but around the 50-60 km mark, I knew that I was going to be in trouble if I didn't get some more food into me. I didn't have any energy gels with me like I usually do, and I had not put any drink mix in my bottles that would give me electrolytes. I hadn't brought any money along either so I could stop and buy more food and drink—which was a big mistake. I started thinking about who I knew that was close to the route I was traveling. I then went off my planned route by a few kilometers to stop by a friend's house for some much needed nourishment. I told them my need and they provided me with a Snickers chocolate bar, which I absolutely love, and a bottle of Gatorade. My friends saved the day for me on that ride. I now had enough fuel in the tank to complete the ride.

The worst time of bonking that I have ever experienced occurred several years ago. I was training for an 8-hour race that I was planning to do solo. In these longer endurance events, you can enter as a team where you take turns

Chapter 5 — Eat

doing laps for the duration of the race; or you can choose to do it solo, where you complete as many laps as you can in the allotted time. I set out on my mountain bike for a long ride one day, on the rail trails in my area. I had lots of drink, food, and some money to buy more if needed. I rode from Kitchener to Cambridge, to Paris, and on to Brantford. From there, I continued on towards Hamilton and was within 20 km of Hamilton when I turned around. I was at 80 km at this point, so I knew my round trip total would be 160 km, which was my goal. I was feeling pretty good during this ride, but I knew I needed to stop and get some more food and drink when I came through Brantford on the return trip.

The ride was going well until I got back to Cambridge and had about 25 km left in my journey to get back home. I started to get that feeling in my stomach, which I know comes from not having enough food and drink. This feeling, which I call "my stomach turning on me," can come from lack of food and drink, too much food and drink, or not the right combination of food and drink. It is an awful feeling in your stomach; and, if not addressed early enough, your day is ruined as far as riding your bike goes.

Every rider has to figure this out for themselves: what kinds of foods and drinks; and how much, or how little, works best for their body. What works for someone else may not necessarily work for you. This has been an interesting process for me as I try different things to see what my body likes the best.

On this particular day, I had one energy gel left, so I took that and thought I would be able to get home fine. The last few kilometers were very difficult, and I was pedaling very slowly. I am very stubborn, though, much to my wife's dismay, so I kept going instead of calling for help and having someone come and pick me up. When I got home I stood in my garage in great levels of discomfort.

Chapter 5 — Eat

As described earlier in the definition of bonking I had an overwhelming sense of fatigue. My stomach really turned on me at this point, and I started vomiting. It was an awful way to end a ride! Shortly after that, I was able to start eating again, slowly. With some rest and some food, I was feeling better within a few hours.

I have seen people push themselves so hard in a race that they throw up at the side of the trail during the race. One time I threw up while taking a break in an endurance race and later fainted. In this particular case I may have had a flu bug that played a part in this. I have had my stomach turn on me in several longer endurance type events. When this has happened, the rest of my participation in that event was severely, negatively affected. Sometimes, it has taken several days for my body to return to normal, in terms of appetite, after these kinds of occurrences.

Now, I know this may seem ridiculous to push yourself to limits that cause your body to respond this way. If we are going to find out what our bodies are capable of doing, sometimes they will be pushed beyond what they can handle. There are many endurance events in a variety of different sports. At the heart of each of these events is the desire to push your body to it limits.

Preparation

I have found several keys in all of this. Number one—can I learn how to better prepare my body for these times? Can I learn to recognize the signs my body is giving me as to how it is doing? As well, can I adjust my efforts so I stay within what I have learned my limits are? This learning has been somewhat slow for me; as I said I am stubborn, and I like to think I am capable of more than the reality has shown that I am. This is where my wife has come in and helped in the learning process. This is just what every husband

Chapter 5 — Eat

likes—when they have to admit that their wife is right!

The other factor to note here, besides the proper fuelling of energy to your body through food, is the value in being properly hydrated before, during, and after a race. If you don't drink enough during a race or ride, your body will scream out to you that something is wrong. This comes most commonly in the form of muscle cramps. I have seen these cramps take people right out of a race because they are in such pain they can't continue. I have also seen people get the shakes and start to get the chills on a hot day while still riding. All of this can come from being dehydrated. You need to be well-hydrated before a race and then keep that hydration at a good level during the race as well.

Every race is different as to how much one should drink. The biggest factor in this is the temperature on race day. This will dictate how much you sweat during the race. The big thing to remember about hydration during a race is that you don't wait to take a drink until you're thirsty. Keep drinking at regular intervals throughout the race, and most times you will be fine.

I have learned to develop good habits with regard to regularly drinking water throughout the day. This becomes a whole life thing, not just a race day thing. Just as eating well needs to become a lifestyle, so is staying well-hydrated. The more serious someone is about their races determines how strict they are about their food and drink intake. If someone is trying to make the Olympics, they will be much more diligent in following a strict diet than what I am as a "weekend warrior"—a term given to those us of who work at normal jobs and race on weekends.

The point in all of this is that everything is connected. I cannot feed my body junk for 5 days a week and then expect to eat well the day before

Chapter 5 — Eat

a race to get good results. Some people I know don't eat well but still get decent results in races. They are able to achieve this because they have been blessed with a lot of talent. With discipline and hard work, these talented people could achieve so much more. Over the long haul, in mountain bike racing, the person who works the hardest and is the most disciplined will usually get the best results.

Spiritual Food

As we journey through life as followers of Jesus, how we feed ourselves spiritually will determine how well we run the race. How do we feed ourselves spiritually? I would like to suggest to you that this happens by living in relationship with God our Father, Jesus the Son, and Holy Spirit. As we live each day in this relationship, we feed our spirits.

In John 4, when the disciples of Jesus were

concerned that He needed something to eat for His physical body, Jesus used this moment to teach them an important thing. Jesus says in John 4:34:

> "My food," said Jesus, "is to do the will of him who sent me and to finish his work.

When we live in this relationship with our Father God, we find out what His will is and then seek to do His will here on Earth. This provides fuel and nourishment to our spirits, and we are able continue on to do what Jesus says in this verse—to finish the Father's work here on Earth.

Another big part of living in this relationship is regularly reading God's Word, the Bible. The Scriptures are the wonderful Word of God that has been given to us. Through this, we get to know what God has done, what He is like, and how much He loves us. The Bible gives us direction that is helpful for everyday living. It is like an owner's manual that has instructions about everything related to the Christian life.

Chapter 5 — Eat

I was taught, at a young age, the value of reading and memorizing the Scriptures. My parents modeled this to me, and I learned it well in the church that I attended while growing up. Over the years, I have memorized many verses of the Bible. These verses that are in my memory bank, as well as others I read daily, continue to provide strength and energy for the journey. Many times, I am reminded of a verse from the Bible at just the time that I need to hear it. These verses can provide encouragement, correction, and direction at the perfect time.

Here are some verses I love about the value of getting the Word of God into you.

Psalm 1:1-3

Blessed is the one who does not walk in step with the wicked or stand in the way that sinners take or sit in the company of mockers, [2] but whose delight is in the law of the Lord, and who meditates on his law day and night.
[3] That person is like a tree planted by streams

of water which yields its fruit in season and whose leaf does not wither—whatever they do prospers.

In these verses, it mentions delighting in the law of the Lord and meditating on it day and night. This will lead to a blessed and prosperous life. How do we meditate on God's word day and night? We can only do this by getting it into us so that we know it so well that we know what it says. This is one of the main reasons I have memorized so many verses of the Bible. Having Scripture memorized is like having energy gels in your pocket when riding. You have all that you need within reach to make it through everything that you face.

Psalm 119:11

I have hidden your word in my heart that I might not sin against you.

This verse talks more about getting the word of God into us. Here the benefit mentioned is

Chapter 5 — **Eat**

that it will keep us from sinning. In that moment when we are tempted to sin, the word of God that we have hidden in us will come to our minds and keep us on track.

> Psalm 119:105
>
> Your word is a lamp for my feet, a light on my path.

The word of God serves as a light to guide us through life. Sometimes, we race our bikes at night; and the only way we can do this is with a good light that shows us the way. If the light goes out, we are in big trouble. I have participated in a 24 hour race the last number of years. This past year, on one of my night laps, a guy rode almost the whole lap behind me because his light had gone out. My light was bright enough for both of us to find our way through the darkness to the finish line. God's word guides us through the dark times and can help us to help others through these difficult times as well.

I would like to suggest to you that we have a spiritual glycogen level. Just as our bodies have stored up energy (glycogen), so, spiritually, we can store up energy that will help us run our race. Some days are easy, and everything is going great. It could be like riding a bike down an easy hill, where you can coast and not spend much energy. Other days are tough, and life seems uphill battle all the way. Our success in these times is related to how much spiritual glycogen we have stored up from our relationship with God and His Word. Just as with our physical bodies, what we feed our bodies determines the outcome of a race; so how well we feed ourselves spiritually will be a factor in how well we run the race of life.

Spiritual Hydration

A couple of other verses to take note of here are:

John 4:13-14

[13] Jesus answered, "Everyone who drinks this water will be thirsty again, [14] but whoever drinks

Chapter 5 — Eat

> the water I give them will never thirst. Indeed, the water I give them will become in them a spring of water welling up to eternal life."

John 7:37-38

> ³⁷ On the last and greatest day of the festival, Jesus stood and said in a loud voice, "Let anyone who is thirsty come to me and drink. ³⁸ Whoever believes in me, as Scripture has said, rivers of living water will flow from within them."

These verses tell us how to be well-hydrated spiritually. As we follow Jesus and live in relationship with Him, our thirst is quenched. Jesus is the living water! We are told, in these verses, that we, actually, will have a well, springing up inside of us and streams will flow from us. How handy would this be if it happened this way in the physical? I would never run out of water again on a long ride!

God has provided everything we need for the race we are in, in this life. It is up to each one of us to access all that has been made available to us. If we do, we will not grow weary or faint be able to run strong to the end!

> *Reflection:*
>
> - What is the 'food' that sustains you right now?
>
> - Is it healthy for you physically, emotionally and spiritually?
>
> - Will it sustain you in the long haul?
>
> - What changes may you need to make for optimal energy in your life?

Chapter 6
ENDURE TO THE END

There comes a time in almost every race that I have done, where I just want to quit. Life would be a whole lot easier if I hadn't decided to participate in this event! "Why am I doing this to myself?" I ask. Do I really want to push past the pain I am experiencing? Can I make it to the end of the race?

The Pain

In the shorter races that I do, this doesn't happen all the time; but the longer the race is, there is always a battle to stay in the race and ride strong to the end. No matter how long the race, though, if I'm racing to the best of my ability and pushing myself to limits, then there is some pain that will be happening in my body. My muscles may be hurting in my legs: my heart rate may be quite high; I may be having a hard time catching my breath; there may be pain in my back; and my hands may be cramping from holding onto the bars. I have had cramps in parts of my body that I didn't know could cramp. My body is drenched with sweat. There may be some things not working quite right on my bike; I may have wiped out and have blood running down my leg. The list of possible reasons I may want to quit goes on and on.

There are exceptions to this, because, on some days, you can push as hard as you want and

Chapter 6 — Endure to the End

it seems easy. This is rare; and, most of the time, how well you deal with pain and suffering is a big part of winning or, at least, competing well in a bike race.

It has been said that it isn't the person that has the best fitness that wins the race, but the one who is willing to suffer the most, that will prevail. If you watch races in the world of professional cycling, like the Tour de France, you will hear the commentators talk about this regularly. What sets the racers who win regularly apart from all the other riders is they are willing to suffer through the pain more than everyone else.

At some level, you need to learn to love the pain or love to hurt. This may sound odd to you if you haven't pushed your body to its limits, but it really is true.

The ability, or shall we say the willingness, to endure is the key to being successful at mountain bike racing. The word 'endure' is defined as "persist for a specified period of time or face and withstand with courage." In a race, when I'm hurting and I wonder why I am doing this, it is my level of my determination to endure that will determine my answer to that question.

I have seen people in racing that regularly do not finish races. Sometimes, these racers may be in great shape physically from lots of training; but they aren't able to battle through the challenges that they face during a race very well. The commitment to endure is the often the difference between winning and losing, or even just finishing or dropping out of the race.

I heard a quote from the world's most famous and now infamous cyclist, Lance Armstrong, which has helped me finish a lot of races when I wanted to quit. Lance said this:

"Pain is temporary, quitting is forever."

I have done quite a few longer endurance

Chapter 6 — Endure to the End

races. In every one of these races, I have wanted to quit at some point during the race. When I am at that point, I remind myself that, if I quit today, I will regret it tomorrow. I choose to push through the temporary pain so that I can finish the race. Later, when I think back, I am glad that I pushed through the pain; and I have no regrets because I endured.

When I am training for my races, I also experience pain that I need to endure. There is another helpful tip that I heard a few years ago that has helped me a lot with my training. The tip is this:

"You race like you train."

I can't just show up on race day and expect good results without having put in the hard work in training. If only it was that easy! If I don't push myself hard in my training and learn to love the hurt and pain when it comes to a race I will not achieve the results I am capable of. When I am training by myself and need motivation to push myself harder I say to myself:

> **"You race like you train".**

Here are a few other thoughts to consider about training that will help us to endure. The best way to get faster as mountain biker is to train with people that are faster than you. This helps us to push ourselves much harder than we tend to do when we train by ourselves. This can also help to simulate race type situations where we may experience pain and hopefully we increase our ability to endure.

The Plan

The more focused we are in our training, the better the results will be. The words of Paul in 1 Corinthians 9:24-27 bears repeating here.

> [24] Do you not know that in a race all the runners run, but only one gets the prize? Run in such

Chapter 6 — Endure to the End

> a way as to get the prize. ²⁵ Everyone who competes in the games goes into strict training. They do it to get a crown that will not last, but we do it to get a crown that will last forever. ²⁶ Therefore I do not run like someone running aimlessly; I do not fight like a boxer beating the air. ²⁷ No, I strike a blow to my body and make it my slave so that after I have preached to others, I myself will not be disqualified for the prize.

If we just go ride our bike, we will get in good shape. But if we want to do well racing our bikes, we need to have a plan in our training to reach our full potential. There are some specific kinds of things that will help us like, intervals, hill training, long endurance rides, and light spin rides, to name a few. I like how Paul says, in verse 26, that he doesn't run aimlessly or fight like a boxer beating the air. No, we need to have a plan and goals when we train. Then we will reach our full potential and have better endurance for the race.

There is also needs to be a good balance

between training and rest/recovery times. We all need time to rest and recover from hard races or training sessions. Every person is unique in how much rest they need. It takes some time to figure out what works best for each of us individually. Some people seem to get stronger the more days in a row they train hard. For example, in a 3 week race like the Tour de France, you will regularly hear the commentators say about some riders, that they seem to get stronger in the 3rd week of the race. While some need to have several rest days or easy days leading up to races, I know my daughter, Samantha, had some of her best races when she did large training blocks for several days leading up to a race.

We each need to figure out what works best for us to get the best results on race day. This balance between rest and training is key in helping us endure during the race.

Chapter 6 — Endure to the End

The Finish

What is the goal of enduring? It is to make it to the end of the race. I not only want to make it to the finish line, but to finish as strongly as possible.

The finish line is the end goal of every race. There have only been a couple of times that I have not made the finish line in a race. There is a very strong determination in me that I will finish every race, no matter what, so I can avoid the dreaded DNF beside my name in the results.

One time, about 5 km into a 24 km mountain bike race, I had a major mechanical issue with my bike. The spring, in the rear derailleur, that tensions the chain broke. At first, I thought my race over; but then I realized that I could still ride my bike if I stayed in a certain gear. This, somehow, took most of the slack out of the chain so I could, at least, pedal the bike. My bike had now become a single speed! This gear was great for climbing hills but not so great for the fast, flat sections of the course (I could coast down the hills, so that was good). I was just happy that I could still be in the race. I finished the race and didn't even finish in last place!

We want to endure to the end. I would say, in a mountain bike race, that no-one is remembered by how well they did in a race, if they didn't make it to the end. No, we are remembered by how well we finish the race and, sometimes, by just the fact that we finished. The goal of every race is to finish!

I have seen many people who have been doing really well in a race never make it to the finish line. I have also seen many who have been having a great race, when something happens that severely hinders their ability to continue, but, somehow, they make it to the finish line. These

Chapter 6 — Endure to the End

are some of the most memorable races. I have seen people limping to the finish line because of a crash that wrecked their bike and hurt their body. I have also seen people running their bike or walking slowly with their bike to the finish with various parts missing or broken.

The story that stands out the most to me comes from a World Cup race that I was privileged to be watching in Windham NY in 2012. The Elite Women were racing and an American named Georgia Gould was having an awesome race. She was leading for most of the race and on the last lap had a good gap on the riders in 2nd and 3rd. It looked like she would win a World Cup race for the first time and in front of the home crowd.

I was standing close to the finish line and looking up the hill where we could see the riders coming. I saw Georgia stop and try to quickly put some air in her rear tire before she entered the last bush section. She got back on the bike quickly and kept going. I thought this couldn't be happening to her. She came out of the bush towards the finish line and we could see she was riding a completely flat rear tire. There was a slight incline just before the finish line and Georgia had to dismount and run with her bike. Now, because the flat tire had slowed her down, the 2nd and 3rd place riders were almost caught up. As Georgia ran towards to the finish line, the other two riders passed her; and she finished in 3rd place.

This was the strangest finish I have ever seen at a mountain bike race! The riders who finished in 1st and 2nd didn't celebrate that much, and all the focus was on the heartbreak of the 3rd place finisher. Georgia was extremely disappointed; but, at least, she finished the race. She had a great race and overcame a major obstacle to, not only finish, but also still finish strong. Yes, she didn't get the win that she was so close to having; but

Chapter 6 — Endure to the End

she did finish.

Many times in our lives, things don't end up the way that we had hoped they would. We could be going along, having a great race, so to speak, and then something happens that has the potential to completely derail us and take us out of the race. How we respond to these challenges will determine much about our lives. Will we have the determination to endure to the end?

Let's look at the passage in Hebrews 12 again for some encouragement.

Hebrews 12:2-3

> [2] fixing our eyes on Jesus, the pioneer and perfecter of faith. For the joy set before him he endured the cross, scorning its shame, and sat down at the right hand of the throne of God. [3] Consider him who endured such opposition from sinners, so that you will not grow weary and lose heart.

Jesus endured a lot when He was on the Earth as a human being. He lived a sinless life, even though he was tempted in every way as we are. Yet, in the end, many hated Him; and they wanted to kill Him. He was brutally beaten and then crucified on a cross. How did He endure all of this? In verse 2, we read that it was because of the joy that was set before Him that He could endure the cross. Jesus had set His sights on the finish line. He knew the goal was to finish what He had set out to do. Because of Jesus' great love for you and me, His goal was to give His life as a ransom for many. He took upon Himself the sins of the world so that you and I can be forgiven of our sins and be restored to relationship with God, our Father.

Jesus is our example of how to endure through difficult times. Verse 3 tells us to consider how Jesus made it through and find encouragement from that so we will not grow weary and lose

Chapter 6 — Endure to the End

heart. I have found that I need to remind myself of this often. If it wasn't easy for Jesus, then why should I expect it to be easy for me?

Do you feel like quitting in some area of your life? Are you not sure how you can go on much longer? I hope that you can find strength and encouragement from these words here to not give up. Just as the willingness to endure to the end is so important in a mountain bike race, so it is in the rest of life. Many times in Scripture, we are encouraged to persevere and not give up.

I remember, a number of years ago, when someone was speaking prophetically into my life. They spoke many encouraging things to me. One of the things they said was that they see diligence in my character and that diligence would be needed to walk out the call that God has on my life. My response to this, as I thought about it, was, "What, you mean this is going to be hard?" Many years have passed since that word was given to me, and I can see that it was very accurate. There is something in me that won't let me give up, and it is what keeps me going. We can call this being stubborn, diligent, or determined; but, whatever it is, I have the willingness to endure to the end.

When we talk of the end, there are two ways to think of this. Of course, there is the final end of our lives here on this Earth when we die. That would most certainly be the ultimate finish line. The other way to think of this is that there are many other finish lines in our lives. These could simply be the end of a day, week, or month, or the end of a specific project we are working on. It could be any goal that we are working toward. Whatever way we think of the term, "the end," I hope that we have determined in our hearts that we will be faithful to endure through what is necessary to get there.

Chapter 6 — Endure to the End

Course Change

One other part to this whole thought of enduring to the end is that, sometimes, it just can't happen. In some bike races, I have seen people completely destroy their bike or be taken off the course on a stretcher. In these cases, there was no way for them to endure to the end of that race. In most cases, these people have come back to try again at another race.

In those smaller finish lines we previously mentioned, we sometimes don't make it to the finish line. I know that, in my own life, I have not finished everything that I have started. This has happened for a whole variety of reasons. Sometimes, it may be something I was never supposed to be involved in, in the first place. Sometimes, things run their course; and it is time for a change. The purpose has been served; and, now, a new thing is calling me. I don't want to keep doing what I have always done just because that's what I have always done.

> **Recognizing the seasons in our lives and having the wisdom to know when they are changing is a crucial.**

For me, the key in this is hearing the voice of God. There will always be those who don't like change and those that think things should remain the same as they have always been. If we all thought that way, we would still live in the Stone Age. Society moves forward because of those that are not content with the way things are and come up with ways to make things better.

Each of us needs to hear God speaking to us as we move through life. This is key to enduring to the end in the things we are called to do. If we get this mixed up, we may be involved in way more things than we can possibly handle. In a bike race, I have learned my limits as to how hard I can push myself and still ride strong to the

Chapter 6 — Endure to the End

finish line. It is the same in the rest of life. We can't do everything and help everyone. We need to know what we are called to do and know when we need to make a change.

I want to conclude this chapter with some encouraging words from

2 Timothy 4:6-8

> [6] For I am already being poured out like a drink offering, and the time for my departure is near. [7] I have fought the good fight, I have finished the race, I have kept the faith. [8] Now there is in store for me the crown of righteousness, which the Lord, the righteous Judge, will award to me on that day—and not only to me, but also to all who have longed for his appearing.

The great Apostle Paul was nearing the end of his life when he wrote these words. In verse 7, he makes three statements that would be awesome things for any of us to be able to say at the end of our lives.

> **My goal is that I can declare that I have fought the good fight, I have finished the race and I have kept the faith!**

If this is true, then we can look forward to the crown that is in store for us.

Yes, the prizes we get on this Earth are wonderful; but they are temporary. In the 1 Corinthians 9:24-27 passage that we looked at earlier in this chapter, Paul says these crowns we get here on this Earth will not last. The crowns we get as followers of Jesus will last forever. He goes on to say, in verse 27, that the reason we work hard at these things and endure to the end is so we will not, in any way, be disqualified for the prize.

There is an eternity in Heaven waiting for all of us who follow Jesus. The crowns and prizes given out there will last forever. This whole idea of eternity is hard for our limited minds to understand. Yet, it is certainly worth you and I

Chapter 6 — Endure to the End

investing all that we have into the race that we are running here on this Earth; to be able to stand before God our Father some day and the words, "Well done, My Good and Faithful Servant," will make all that we have gone through worthwhile.

I invite you to join me in determining in your heart that you will endure to end and that, when you fall, you will get back up and keep going.

Reflection:

- Where in your life are you tempted to 'quit running' right now?

- Is marriage hard?

- Your job at a dead end?

- Have a boss that seems to want to make you life miserable?

- What choices can you make to help you endure and keep going?

Chapter 7
EVALUATE

After every race is over, we mountain bikers like to look at the results. (We also like to look at pictures of ourselves racing!) We like to see how we finished and how we did compared to others. Many times, the results are posted at the race; but they are always posted online for us to check out. After an Ontario Cup race, I usually spend a good chunk of time when we get home, going over the results from the race that day. I like to see how I did, what my lap times were, and how I compared to the others I was racing against. I also like to check out how everyone on Two Wheel Racing did that day.

As I look at results from a race, it prompts an evaluation of my performance that day. The evaluation also includes the training and other things that I did leading up to race day. What did I eat the day of the race and the week before? How much rest did I have? Was I stressed or relaxed leading up to the race and on race day? How much and what kind of riding did I do the week before the race?

My improvement as a mountain bike racer depends on how well I do this evaluation after a race. Can I learn more about myself from each race so that I know what works for me and what isn't helpful at all? I have also benefited a great deal over the years from talking with others and getting their input as part of my evaluation.

Chapter 7 — Evaluate

Learning from others is huge and a much better option than trying to figure things out all on my own.

As we go through life, we need to regularly take time to evaluate how we are doing. If we don't take this time to examine ourselves, we, most likely, will keep doing what we have always done, whether it is producing good results or not. A famous quote from Albert Einstein is applicable here. He says:

> **"Insanity is doing the same thing over and over again and expecting different results".**

I almost hesitate to share this quote because it seems so harsh. I also know that, at times in my life, I have been guilty of this. We can get stuck in a rut, and, many times, it just seems easier to keep doing what is familiar to us, even though it isn't working.

We can evaluate ourselves in many areas. We can look at our relationships, physical health, careers, family, finances, and time management, just to name a few. All of these are good; and our time spent reviewing how we are doing and how we can improve, will bring forth great results.

As a follower of Jesus, I like the invitation for God to evaluate us in

Psalms 139:23-24

Search me, God, and know my heart; test me and know my anxious thoughts. [24] See if there is any offensive way in me, and lead me in the way everlasting.

If this is the cry of our hearts to God, we will be changed! In these verses, we are inviting God to search us, to know our hearts and thoughts, to test us and examine us for any offensive way. This will lead us in the way that is everlasting. It seems like a very thorough examination to me.

Chapter 7 — Evaluate

The key to this evaluation being a success is our response to what God reveals to us. If we are shown things, but don't want to change, and we hold on to old habits, we will continue getting the same results. In mountain bike racing, when someone gives me good advice as to how I can improve my racing, I need to make the necessary changes to benefit from this. In the same way, God reveals things to us that need to be changed in our lives. He may show us that our hearts are full of judgment, bitterness, anger, and jealousy. If we let these things go and replace them with love, kindness, and forgiveness, we will be changed.

Evaluating ourselves will not only help us endure to the end of the race it will help us to finish well!

That is my prayer for each one of you that reads this book.

Reflection:

- Take time to evaluate yourself, as suggested in this chapter.

- What are the things in your life that need to change, for you to get better results?

CONCLUSION

Jesus declares that He has come that we may have life and have it to the full (John 10:10). He is calling us out of the ruts in which we are stuck. He calls us into a life full of meaning and purpose as we follow him. It really is a ride that is like nothing else we can experience! When you come into a relationship with the one who created you, all of the sudden, life makes sense. This is why I am here on this Earth: to know God and invite others to know him.

If you don't know Jesus as your Savior and

Lord, I would invite you, today, to make the decision to give your life to Him. In the first chapter of this book, I talked about making the decision to enter the race changes everything. So to deciding to follow Jesus will change your life.

You can start this journey by saying this prayer and believing it with your heart:

Jesus, I confess that I am a sinner. I believe that you died on the cross for my sins and that you rose from the dead. Please forgive me of my sins. I give you my life and ask you to me my Lord. Fill me with your Holy Spirit and help me to tell others about your great love. Thank you that I am now a child of God. Amen!

Congratulations! You are about to start the most amazing adventure of your life. Welcome to the Kingdom of God!

Throughout this book I have touched a lot of different topics, without going too deeply

Conclusion

into them. My hope is that this has gotten you thinking, so that you will continue searching for wisdom in all these areas. Pay attention to the topics that really sparked an interest in you. This is usually an indicator that more attention is needed in this area of your life. My prayer is that Holy Spirit was at work in each of you as you read this book and that this book will produce good fruit in the lives of all who read it.

I hope, as well, that many of you will be inspired to get back on your bicycle and discover the simple pleasure that can come from riding a bike. Dust off that bike that hasn't been used in a while. Rediscover that joy you had as a kid when you first learned to ride.

More About
PAUL & ANGIE WAGLER

Paul Wagler is an author, mentor, coach, and inspired speaker with a gift of encouragement, an approachable way to connect with people, and an awesome ability to quote scripture. An avid cyclist in both mountain bike and road disciplines, Paul also manages the Two Wheel Racing Mountain Bike Team. He has worked in the transportation industry, as a bus operator and truck driver.

Paul and his wife, Angie, are the founders of Arise Now—a ministry to encourage and equip.

They have been church planters and pastors, and have been involved in church in various forms, including traditional, cell, house churches, and leadership healing groups. They understand wilderness pruning and fine-tuning, and have an understanding of walking through the painful process that pre-empts inheritance.

Happily married for almost 30 years, they make their home in Kitchener, Ontario, Canada. They have three grown children and one much-loved dog.

Do check out Paul's other book in this series, *Lessons Learned on the Seat of my Bus*—available in both kindle and paperback versions on Amazon.

Paul and Angie would love to hear how this book has impacted you. You can contact them through their website: **www.arisenow.ca** or the Arise Now facebook page.

ONE LAST THING...

If you enjoyed this book and found it helpful we would love if you would post a short review on Amazon. Thanks!

OTHER BOOKS AVAILABLE
—BY PAUL WAGLER

Lessons Learned on the Seat of my Bus —Volume 1

You will want to read this first book in the Lesson's Learned Series to find out this bus driver's secrets to enjoying life no matter what happens!

Available in both kindle and paperback versions on Amazon.

What others are saying...

Paul writes from such a unique perspective bringing insight and humor into everyday life. Buckle your seat belt and enjoy the ride in reading this treasure.
    —Brian Fleming, Author - "Your Life Matters"

Oh, Paul - you have hit the nail on the head. This book is so much fun! I love "Where you are seated determines your perspective." Each of the sections starts off like a tasty appetizer - and ends up with a nourishing nugget of God's truth. I look forward to your "Seat of the Bicycle" Book.
    —Jane Huff, Author - "An Intimate Look at the Armour of God"

I can't stop laughing from the stories in your book! I'm sitting here alone in the living room just laughing out loud! Good Job!
    —Judith Ann Martin, Blogger, www.HeyJude45.com

—BY ANGIE WAGLER

Go on a journey with Jesus in

All my ROOMS

He is knocking on your door and wanting you to invite him in to all your rooms. Find out what He will say and impart to you that will bring transformation to your heart and life!

Available in kindle and paperback on Amazon.

What others are saying...

Angie Wagler's book *All My Rooms* is a delightfully practical look at life. By comparing a room of your house to a part of your life, she enables you to invite Jesus in and assist you in every way.

The Living Room correlates to our thought processes. The Family Room speaks of relationships, and how to forgive. From The Bedroom: "To sleep well, we need to put fear in its place!" Her personal story of doing this is greatly encouraging.

At the end of each chapter, Angie invites us to take some time to write down our own reaction to her teaching. This engaging book is one you will want to use over and over. Even as we sometimes move from place to place physically and need to "redecorate," at times, we also have to move in our thinking. All My Rooms gives a refreshing way for a spiritual spring cleaning and refocusing of our lives.

—Jane Huff, Author, An Intimate Look at the Armor of God: Finding Safety in a Broken World

Watch also for Volume 2 in the Transformation Series

The **WILDERNESS TRAINING** Manual

a resource to bring freedom from the slavery mindset and to access the promises of God!

CHECK OUT THE
TWO MINUTE WAKE UP CALL

Do you need a Wake Up Call????
It's time to Arise Now! Stay Awake and Stay Alert!

The *Two Minute Wake Up Call* is a video series promoted on Facebook, youtube and through email.

Through these short two minute videos, Paul and Angie offer encouragement and insights to arise now in Jesus, discover God's plan, be filled with passion to live out your purpose.

Join the growing army that is arising now. You can receive these videos by:

1. Signing up at arisenow.ca to have them delivered to your inbox as they are released.
2. Subscribe to the Arise Now youtube channel. And/or
3. Like and follow the Arise Now Facebook page.

Made in the USA
Charleston, SC
16 July 2016